What You
Should Know About
Social Responsibility

D1569104

What You Should Know About Social Responsibility

by
Charles C. Ryrie

Moody Press
Chicago

© 1982 by
THE MOODY BIBLE INSTITUTE
OF CHICAGO

All Scripture quotations, except those noted otherwise, are from the
New American Standard Bible, © 1960, 1962, 1963, 1968, 1971,
1972, 1973, 1975, and 1977 by The Lockman Foundation, and are
used by permission.

The use of selected references from various versions of the Bible in
this publication does not necessarily imply publisher endorsement of
those versions in their entirety.

Library of Congress Cataloging in Publication Data

Ryrie, Charles Caldwell, 1925-
    What you should know about social responsibility.

    1. Social ethics. 2. Christian ethics. 3. Social problems. I. Title.
HM216.R95   170   81-16804
ISBN 0-8024-9417-X   AACR2

Printed in the United States of America

Contents

Chapter One

Salt and Light

Salt and Light

"You are the salt of the earth. . . . You are the light of the world" (Matthew 5:13-14). So said the Lord about His disciples.

But what does it mean to be salt and light? Clear as the question seems to be, the answers are, to say the least, not uniform. For some, being salt and light means playing a role in the world that will ultimately renovate it, bringing in the kingdom or nearly so.

For others, being salt and light focuses on more limited objectives. Being salt and light means being against abortion or homosexuality. Or it means supporting certain political candidates, or adopting a more simplified life-style, or feeding the hungry and distributing the wealth more evenly.

Of course, not all agree on what movements are legitimate or which one or ones should be given priority. Some who actively try to relieve poverty and hunger would back away from redistributing the wealth.

This divergence of answers surfaces an important theological question: What is the relation of the Christian's social responsibility to the gospel? Is saving souls the gospel, or is saving souls plus saving bodies the "whole" gospel? Is God's plan of redemption saving souls alone, or is social action also redemptive?

Movements come and go. Therefore, what movements a Christian ought to be concerned about could never be so important as the gospel. If social responsibility is a part of the content of the gospel it must have top priority. If it is not, then the believer must think carefully about his priorities and arrange the various opportunities of his life in biblical order. What priority should be given to social responsibilities in comparison, say, to church responsibilities, or family responsibilities, or the cultivation of personal holiness? Answers do not come readily, for many voices call for the believer's time, interest, and money.

Discerning God's will comes from an understanding of God's Word. We must examine what God's Word says about this area of social responsibility.

What is salt that has become tasteless? What will light do for those on whom it casts its rays? What is the gospel? How did Christ face the social evils of His day? What can a single individual do in the face of worldwide shortages? What should he do? Is the triumph of evil inevitable? Is there a Christian stand on issues?

These are some of the questions connected with being salt and light. What are the biblical answers?

10

Chapter Two

What Are Social Ethics?

What Are
Social Ethics?

The journey we are about to take leads us into the field of social ethics—that is, the problems of society and an individual's relation to them.

The English word *ethics* comes from a Greek word that means "custom, usage, habit," and is used in a familiar verse in the New Testament: "Bad company corrupts good morals" (1 Corinthians 15:33). The word translated *morals* is the word *ethics.*

Ethics can be related to personal standards of morality or to morals in society. The former is called personal ethics and the latter, social ethics. The latter, social ethics, will occupy our attention in this book. When our Lord said, "You are to be perfect, as your heavenly Father is perfect" (Matthew 5:48), He was speaking about personal ethics. When He commanded, "Render to Caesar the things that are Caesar's" (Matthew 22:21), He was speaking about a social ethic.

In the late 1940s when the movement known as New Evangelicalism set forth its manifesto, one of its main concerns was to do something about the social implications of the gospel, that, in the opinion of the new evangelicals, fundamentalists had abandoned. A generation later, in the 1970s, the new evangelicals were labeled "establishment evangelicals" by a newer group called the young evangelicals, who, according to their own publicity, were the only ones with a genuine social concern. They said:

> We have found social concern among Establishment Evangelicals to be often merely an offering of pious words rather than a demonstration of prophetic action. Hence, if we are looking for a powerful expression of spiritual renewal in Orthodox Christianity—one genuinely committed to reconciliation and active faith in a secular society—we shall have to search elsewhere. [Richard Quebedeaux, *The Young Evangelicals* (New York: Harper & Row, 1974), p. 37]

The International Congress on World Evangelization held in Lausanne in 1974 devoted an entire article in its covenant to Christian social responsibility. Some felt the statement should have made it clearer that social concern is a part of evangelism, while others seemed to regret that it did not make clear that this concern was not a part of evangelism. The debate continues, often centering on the question, what is the whole gospel? Those who feel that social ethics are not a part of the gospel are accused of mutilating the gospel, and those who feel that social concern is a

14

part of the gospel are charged with preaching another gospel.

Social ethics is a relevant subject because it is biblical, and everything in the Bible is relevant whether we think so or not. It is timely, since it continues to evoke so much discussion. It is serious, because if social concern is really a part of the gospel, then we must give it a priority it really has not had in the thinking and living of most evangelicals.

Social ethics must be positioned properly on a scale of priorities of Christian responsibilities. Fortunately, even though evangelicals cannot agree on this scale of priorities, in practice almost all evangelicals do concern themselves with some aspects of social ethics. Those who believe that the gospel concerns evangelism only are usually not uninvolved in the social problems of their world. Likewise, those who campaign for more involvement are usually not unconcerned about evangelism. Generally it is not a question of involvement versus noninvolvement. It is a question of the degree of involvement and the areas of involvement. The evangelical who demonstrates for capital punishment and the evangelical who rallies against it are both involved; both feel that they have biblical support for their opposite viewpoints. The evangelical who protests military conscription and the one who supports it are both involved in a social issue, and again, both feel their positions are biblical. The evangelical who campaigns for a conservative political candidate and the one who campaigns against him are both involved in the political arena, and both feel justified in their respective positions. Both sides are involved, but their agendas are hardly the same.

Furthermore, evangelicals are much more involved than the general public. Eighty-one percent say they do volunteer work for the church or some religious organization, as opposed to 40 percent in the general population. Thirty percent give directly to the poor, as compared to 19 percent of the general public, and 42 percent say they are involved in social activities, as compared with 27 percent generally (*Christianity Today,* 19 September 1980, p. 27).

The only definitive guidelines for answering the question of how, where, and to what degree evangelicals should be involved are found in the Bible.

Chapter Three

What Is the Gospel?

What Is the Gospel?

Basic to the question of what priority should be given to social action is the matter of what is included in the gospel.

If the content of the gospel is evangelism, then social responsibility is not a part of it. If the gospel includes obedience, following Christ, bringing in the kingdom or at least living kingdom ethics now, then social responsibilities will definitely be a part of the gospel message.

Usually the options are not stated so sharply. Many speak about the primacy of evangelism, but to do that is to include in the gospel things other than the salvation message. If something is primary, it has to be primary in relation to other items on a list. The total list would be, in that

19

case, the components of the gospel. To delete something like social responsibility would then result in a deficient or mutilated gospel.

The "whole" gospel. One hears frequently today this expression "the whole gospel." The Lausanne Covenant, Article 6, states that "world evangelization requires the whole church to take the whole Gospel to the whole world" (J.D. Douglas, ed., *Let the Earth Hear His Voice* [Minneapolis: World Wide Publications, 1975], p. 5). In an address delivered to that convention Rene Padilla said, "I maintain that both of these views [salvation as social or personal] are incomplete gospels and that the greatest need of the church today is the recovery of the full Gospel of our Lord Jesus Christ—the whole Gospel for the whole man for the whole world" (ibid., p. 144). Thus in his view, a gospel that only focuses on the eternal salvation of the individual is an incomplete gospel.

Let us examine this claim by studying how the New Testament uses the word *gospel.*

The Greek word translated *gospel* means "good news." Good news about what? The answer to that question will come from the particular passage where the word occurs and may differ in various places. For instance, it may refer to a non-redemptive good news as in 1 Thessalonians 3:6 where Timothy's report to Paul of the steadfastness of the new converts in Thessalonica was good news, a gospel. Or it may designate a false gospel as in Galatians 1:6 which the Judaizers were promoting as good news. Or it may refer to good news about the coming kingdom (Matthew 4:23), or the good news about the death and resurrection of Christ (1 Corinthians 15:1).

In Matthew the word *gospel* is used all but once concerning the good news about the coming kingdom (4:23; 9:35; 24:14). The last reference shows clearly that the kingdom did not come during Jesus' lifetime since the good news about it is still to be proclaimed in the future. However, when Mary anointed the Lord in anticipation of His death and burial, the Lord said that wherever this gospel (good news about His death) was preached, her good deed would also be known (Matthew 26:13).

Mark's use of the term *gospel* uniformly emphasizes the person of Christ (1:1, 14-15; 8:35; 10:29; 13:10; 14:9; 16:15). He is the central theme of the good news. Luke also uses the word *gospel* to underscore the centrality of Christ to the good news (2:10) as well as announcing the kingdom (4:43). But one reference in Luke (4:18-19) is particularly important to the question of social responsibility. On this occasion in the synagogue in Nazareth the Lord said: "THE SPIRIT OF THE LORD IS UPON ME, BECAUSE HE ANOINTED ME TO PREACH THE GOSPEL TO THE POOR. HE HAS SENT ME TO PROCLAIM RELEASE TO THE CAPTIVES, AND RECOVERY OF SIGHT TO THE BLIND, TO SET FREE THOSE WHO ARE DOWNTRODDEN, TO PROCLAIM THE FAVORABLE YEAR OF THE LORD." Social activists use these verses to define the Christian's mission as bettering the situation of the poor and downtrodden. A proper understanding of the passage, however, depends upon the meanings of *gospel* and *poor.*

Who are the poor? They may be the materially poor or the spiritually poor. Or both. Poor can refer to the economically deprived (Luke 14:13, 21; 16:20; 18:22). Our Lord did preach the gospel to the poor (Luke 7:22), but He also preached to the rich (Luke 5:32; 10:1-10).

Poor can also refer to spiritual poverty (Matthew 5:3; Revelation 3:17). So conceivably the Lord was announcing that His ministry would be to those who were spiritually bankrupt.

21

Or perhaps He was saying both. That is, He came to announce good news to both the spiritually and materially poor, which, of course, He did. In the verse itself, Luke 4:18, both actual and figurative ideas seem to be combined. Healing the brokenhearted seems to be both actual and figurative. Preaching deliverance to the captives seems to be figurative, referring to those captured by sin. Our Lord certainly did not release those actually held captive by the Roman authorities. He did restore actual sight to some blind people, and He announced good news to those who were blind spiritually. So the word *poor* may refer both to those who were poor materially and spiritually.

What is the gospel He proclaimed? We have already seen that primarily our Lord preached the good news about the coming kingdom. In that kingdom, yet to be established, there will be spiritual and material deliverance. People get sidetracked when they attempt to impose kingdom ethics on the world today without the physical presence of the King. The Christian is responsible to practice church ethics, not kingdom ethics. Church ethics focus on the church; kingdom ethics focus on the world.

But even if you do not agree with what I have just said, it remains clear that the Lord's mission was to preach the gospel. That is the message that will benefit the poor.

John does not use the word *gospel* at all. In Acts, Luke records the dissemination of the good news, but it is Paul who gives us the technical definition of the word as it relates to us today. The classic passage is 1 Corinthians 15:3-8. Christ's death and resurrection are, literally, "of first importance." The good news is based on two facts: a Savior died and He lives. The mention of Christ's burial proves the reality of His death. He

22

did not merely swoon only to be revived later. He actually died. The list of witnesses (vv. 5-8) proves the reality of His resurrection. He *died* and was buried (the proof); He *rose* and was seen (the proof). Christ's death and resurrection are the foundations of the gospel of the grace of God. Notice the same twofold emphasis in Romans 4:25: He "was delivered up . . . and raised . . ." Everyone who believes that good news is saved (1 Corinthians 15:2). That, and that alone, is the whole gospel of the grace of God.

What about other responsibilities? If, as some insist, the gospel must also include social responsibility in order to be a whole gospel, then why could it not also be said that it must include other Christian responsibilities? Why stop with social responsibility? Why not include church responsibilities or family responsibility? Who decides what responsibilities are part of the whole gospel and which ones are not?

Evangelism by its very meaning (announcing the evangel or good news) cannot include other responsibilities since the good news does not. Futhermore, it is inaccurate to speak about the message of spiritual salvation having primacy in our mission as if other messages (like social responsibility) are a part, albeit a lesser one, of evangelism. Other responsibilities are part of our Christian duty, but they are not a part of Christian evangelism.

What is our commission? Is our commission evangelism and teaching, as has been understood historically, or is it evangelism and social action? John R. W. Stott has said: "I now see more clearly that not only the consequences of the commission but the actual commission itself must be understood to include social as well as evangelistic responsibility . . ." (John R. W. Stott, *Christian Mission in the Modern World* [Downers

23

Grove, Ill.: Inter-Varsity, 1975], p. 23). He leans heavily on John 20:21 and reduces the commission to that of service. As the Lord was sent to serve so we are sent to serve.

That in itself is not wrong unless service is wrongly defined. Was our Lord's service social or redemptive? Obviously redemptive. He came to redeem. But, it may be asked, did He not also do social service? The answer is: very selectively, almost within the community of Israel, and never oriented toward politics or economic redistribution. Further, His good deeds like the miracles were proofs of His ability to redeem.

To be sure, God is a God of justice as well as redemption, as Stott and others say, but it is not true to imply that God's program *today* is to effect worldwide justice as well as worldwide preaching of the gospel. Justice will come to this world only when Christ comes, and in the meantime, we are to evangelize and teach. But Stott and others would have believers give high priority to economic equality, political activism against war and nuclear weapons, and industrial justice. All of these causes, they say, are part of the commission.

Not so. The gospel is the good news that our Lord Jesus Christ died for our sins and rose again from the dead. All who believe in Him have eternal life. The commission to the church is to preach that good news and to teach the Word. The consequences of obeying the Word are manifold.

Chapter Four

God's Character and Social Problems

God's Character and Social Problems

Our concept of God is central to everything, certainly to the practice of both personal and social ethics. People of all theological persuasions recognize that, even though they do not all have the same view of God nor do they all consistently apply their concept of God to the problems of life.

To the liberal, love seems to be the only attribute of God for all practical purposes. Ideas of God's justice and righteousness are dissolved into love. Though evangelicals recognize that God exhibits a number of attributes in addition to love, they are not always clear as to which attributes relate to social problems and what those attributes teach us about God's view toward social needs.

God is sovereign. The fact that God is sovereign does not mean that He is a dictator. Basically it means that God is the supreme ruler. The word *sovereign* does not of itself tell us how He rules. But the Bible does. He rules by working all things after the counsel of His own will (Ephesians 1:11).

In doing that, He sometimes directly intervenes, as when He elected Israel to be His chosen people. That decision carried with it a number of social ramifications for both Israel and the rest of the world. Sometimes He intervenes by sending rain on one city and not on another as punishment (Amos 4:7). In the future He will send worldwide judgments that will bring all kinds of social problems.

Sometimes God permits men to have free rein over their sinful desires, again with far-reaching social ramifications (Romans 1). In the realm of politics we know that God raises up and removes rulers (Daniel 4:35), sometimes by direct intervention (Acts 12:23) and sometimes by permitting them to carry out their sinful plans (Revelation 13:5-7). But He is in control of all things.

Let me raise a problem. If God should judge some area by withholding rain and bringing famine, could it be possible that well-meaning Christians might be dulling the sword of God's judgment if they attempted to alleviate the famine? That's a tough question, but it illustrates how an attempt to reflect the love of God might counter the justice of God. Discharging one's social responsibility by reflecting the attributes of God calls for a great deal of discernment on the part of the Christian.

God is love. God is love, but what is love? It is seeking the highest good in the object loved, and ultimately good is whatever brings glory to God. So love is seeking the glory of God.

28

When the Bible says that God is love, then it means that He glorifies Himself, without any suggestion of selfishness or pride. When the Bible tells us to love one another, we are to seek the glory of God in each other's lives. When we are told to love those outside the family of God, we are to seek God's glory in their lives. Reflecting the love of God in any responsibility will result in glorifying God.

Immediately this concept of the love of God tells us something about priorities in relation to the unsaved. To love those outside the family of God (that is, to glorify God in their lives) means primarily to seek their salvation; for when a person is saved, he begins a display of the glory of God that will continue throughout all eternity (Ephesians 2:7). Every attribute of God as reflected in the life of a Christian brings glory to Him, but perhaps none as much as the display of His grace in the salvation of a person. As believers win the lost and they in turn display the grace of God, this becomes the highest form of showing the love of God.

Doing good to all men also displays the love of God. But those good works, no matter what they are, can never be as important as winning the lost.

God is good. God's goodness is seen in many facets of common grace: in nature (Matthew 5:45), in the arrangement of seasons so that we may have food to eat (Acts 14:17), in restraining sin and exposing men to the gospel (John 16:8-11). God is even "kind to ungrateful and evil men" (Luke 6:35).

But why is God so good? So that people will come to repentance (Romans 2:4).

If we then seek to reflect the goodness of God by giving good gifts to people, even undeserving ones, it should be with the aim of leading them to

29

salvation in Christ.

God is just. His justice will ultimately triumph. Some say that means that Godlike action on the part of Christians will be concerned with establishing justice in the world now: justice for the poor by dividing the wealth; justice for the oppressed by any means, including (in the opinion of some) violent revolution. Often cited as proof is Micah 6:8: "And what does the Lord require of you but to do justice, to love kindness, and to walk humbly with your God?" But these are personal requirements, not programs for social action. To do justice is quite different from imposing justice. God's righteous judgments are often delayed for higher purposes known only to Him. It is not necessarily the will of God to bring immediate justice to people.

That is not to say that God delights in injustice, but it is to say that He often tolerates scoffers and rebels who inflict injustices on others because He is "not wishing for any to perish, but for all to come to repentance" (2 Peter 3:9).

Justice has several aspects. There is an ultimate justice that God Himself will bring about. There is a present justice that can sometimes be accomplished and sometimes not. There is a postponed justice that is often involuntary and sometimes used by God for higher purposes. The believer may not always be certain when he should fight for immediate justice, or when he must grieve over justice that must be postponed and wait patiently for God's ultimate justice.

Consider these situations. A Christian worker is not being treated fairly by his employer. He seeks redress through his union. A Christian citizen is being defrauded by his government. He seeks redress in the courts. Or a Christian's neighbor is violating something in the city code.

30

The Christian registers a complaint with the proper city officials. All of these actions are legitimate avenues of protest. All the actions are just. But they might be wrong actions. By insisting on immediate justice, the worker, the citizen, or the homeowner may alienate those against whom he has the just grievance and lose opportunities for witness. Contrariwise, not to insist on legitimate rights may also alienate those people and make them scoff at any witness. Either action might open or close the door to gospel witness. In other words, it is not always easy to decide if we should insist on justice because God is just, or deny our rights because God is longsuffering.

To say that "Christian social concern imitates God's concern" (David Moberg, *Inasmuch* [Grand Rapids: Eerdmans, 1965], p. 32) is little more than a platitude that says little theologically or practically. For theologically God's concern is sometimes expressed in love that is kind, and other times in love that is harsh. Sometimes it is expressed in goodness that tolerates evil and other times in justice that does not.

How will the believer know which is the proper course of social action at a particular time? Only through intimate fellowship with the living Lord will he know what to do in each situation. And that is a much more difficult procedure than some well-planned, universal course of action. God's nature is multi-faceted and His attributes are many. So our imitation of Him must be Spirit-directed, or it will not be a true representation of His character.

Chapter Five

Man in the Image of God

Man in the
Image of God

Created in the image of God, man is a noble creature. To be sure, sin marred that image but did not totally erase it. Some say that because man's noble potential has been suppressed by adverse social condition, the church should seek to change those conditions and give unsaved people a chance to flourish. But is that what the Bible says?

The meaning of the image of God. Though many definitions are given of the image of God, many of them seem to obscure rather than clarify. Let me suggest a descriptive definition from the creation account in Genesis 1 and 2. It consists of three facets.

1. The image of God in which man was created

includes dominion which God, the supreme sovereign, delegated to man. Genesis 1:26 relates the image to man's ability to rule over the creatures of the earth. But after the Fall his rule was restricted, for after sin entered man was not recommissioned to subdue the earth (Genesis 9:3 compared with 1:26).

2. The image of God also included intelligence (Genesis 2:20). But again, after the Fall his mind was darkened and limited, though the mind of man can still achieve astounding feats.

3. The image of God also included life itself, for it was the living God who created Adam (Genesis 2:7). After sin entered the span of human life was considerably shortened, and man's creative potential that is a part of life was often misdirected. But still man even in his fallen state is a noble creature.

The biblical social ramifications. What does all of this mean? Is it our duty to better man's conditions so that he can realize his full potential? But "full potential" must take into account the fact of the fall of man and his total depravity. Though mankind still experiences a limited sovereignty, intelligence, and life, all the aspects of his being are affected by sin. "Full potential" may involve good deeds (though without saving merit in God's sight), but it may also erupt in the full expression of sinfulness (Romans 1:21-32). But even if conditions were created so that people would only do good, that would not get them to heaven.

What does the Bible say about ramifications of man's being created in the image of God?

The ramifications of being in the image of God. There are at least five.

1. Certainly the Bible teaches that above everything else man needs a Savior. Improving his lot in life will not necessarily make him hap-

36

pier (Are all wealthy people happy and all poor people unhappy?). Seeing to sufficient social security will not cause anyone to live longer. His need of a Savior is paramount.

2. The common ancestry of all in Adam has an important ramification in relation to racial prejudice. Paul said that God made of one blood all nations of men to dwell on the face of the earth and determined the bounds of their habitation (Acts 17:26). Although some have taken the phrase "bounds of their habitation" to support such things as apartheid, proper exegesis forbids such an interpretation. God has determined how long each nation will flourish and what the boundaries of its territory should be.

Since all people are of the same blood and God's offspring by creation, there can be no superior or inferior race of people. The biblical teaching of the solidarity of the race underscores the urgency of evangelism and prohibits all racial or national prejudice.

3. Cursing any other person is forbidden by the doctrine of the image of God. James warns against such treatment of any other human being on the basis that all were created in the image of God and still retain it (3:9). A specific social responsibility that might flow from this would be to campaign against so much that is seen and heard on television that clearly violates James 3:9.

4. The doctrine of man's being created in the image of God was the basis for the original institution of capital punishment. The fact that a murdered person was created in the image of God demands the execution of the murderer (Genesis 9:6). Though there is disagreement as to whether or not Romans 13:4 grants civil government the power to exercise captial punishment today, if it does, believers could well be involved in pro-

37

moting laws that permit it.

5. Paul relates the doctrine of the image of God to a matter of church ethics when he wrote of the uncovering of a man's head in public worship and the covering of a woman's head. The man, he said, should be uncovered because he was made in the image of God; by contrast, a woman should be covered because she is the glory of man (1 Corinthians 11:7). One cannot help but observe that this matter is usually not on anyone's agenda these days, even though its basis in God's original act of creation can scarcely be written off as cultural and inapplicable.

These are the biblical ramifications of man's being created in the image of God, and they do involve specific social responsibilities.

Chapter Six

What We Learn from the Old Testament

What We Learn from
the Old Testament

What the Old Testament contributes to social ethics is not always properly used. Some popular treatments of the subject do little more than refer to a few of the better known prophetic denunciations of injustice and insensitivity to the poor as the basis for stirring up Christian involvement in social problems today. I say "do little more" simply because such an approach is not only overly simplistic but often theologically inept.

Consider this question: Is every command in the Bible binding on all people at all times? If so, then why do we not obey them all today? If not, then which ones should we obey?

Or consider this: Can the laws of a theocracy (which Israel was) be transferred to a democracy or a dictatorship?

Thoughtful reflection on questions like these will help steer a proper course through the Old Testament contribution to this subject.

The concept of a theocracy. A theocracy is defined as "government of a state by immediate divine guidance or by officials regarded as divinely guided." Israel was a theocracy in both senses of this definition. She experienced immediate divine guidance from God, and she was ruled through the mediation of judges, kings, and priests. That distinguished Israel from all the other nations (Deuteronomy 4:8) and placed special responsibility on her to obey those God-given laws (Amos 3:2).

Social responsibilities in the theocracy of Israel. To attempt to list, let alone explain, all the laws of the theocracy belonging to the realm of social ethics would needlessly sidetrack us. A sampling of specific laws within discernably broad categories will give us the necessary information and perspective.

At least three broad categories of social laws are found. These three categories (or four or five, if one finds more) represent a package. The Mosaic code was a unit, though it can be catalogued in various ways. The commandments of Exodus 20 are followed without any break by the judgments of Exodus 21, that in turn are followed without a break by the ordinances of Exodus 25 and following. The New Testament reminds us that to offend in one point of the law is to be guilty of all (James 2:10). Sins of the heart and sins of the hand are despicable to God. Indeed, sins of the heart cause sins of the hand. That is why the sin of idolatry was so contemptible in God's sight, and I list it as the first category because it was so prominent and because it was the cause of other social sins.

42

1. The prohibition of idolatry is one of the three immutable absolutes in Jewish ethics (incest and murder being the other two). The first two commandments of the Decalogue prohibit image worship as well as the worship of any other god (Exodus 20:1-3). Idolatry was punishable by death (Deuteronomy 17:2-7).

The history of idolatry among the Hebrews began with Rachel's stealing Laban's teraphim (Genesis 31:19). During Moses' absence from the camp at Mount Sinai, the people clamored for a visible representation of God, constructed the golden calf, and accompanied their idolatry by singing and dancing naked before the idol (Exodus 32:6, 18-19, 25). The word *play* in 32:6 implies sexual gestures or acts. Later, though commanded to destroy the idols of Canaan, the Israelites rebelled (Judges 2:12, 14), and the Canaanized worship of Yahweh evolved. The Babylonian captivity resulted as a direct punishment for idolatry (Jeremiah 29:8-10).

Some of the practical and social ramifications of idolatry were these: acts of adultery (Hosea 2:13), captivity (Hosea 8:13), unacceptable offerings (Amos 6:1-6), violence, deceit, and shortages of food (Micah 6:12-16). Departure from the true God always leads to deterioration of life. And, of course, that is just as true today (1 John 5:21).

2. A second broad category of social sins in the theocracy concerned oppression of the poor and needy. The Old Testament abounds with exhortations and commands concerning the poor and needy. The Mosaic law protected the poor from unlawful usury charges (Exodus 22:25; Leviticus 25:36). The corners of a field were not to be reaped, nor the vineyards stripped clean of their fruit, in order to leave something for the needy to eat (Leviticus 19:9-10; 23:22). Whatever grew

43

spontaneously in the fields during the sabbatical year was to be left unreaped for the benefit of any who wanted to gather it (Leviticus 25:5). Individuals were permitted to pluck grain or eat grapes belonging to another as long as nothing was carried away (Deuteronomy 23:24-25).

Special blessing was promised those who gave to the poor (Proverbs 19:17; Psalm 41:1), and those who oppressed the poor were singled out for judgment (Psalm 140:12). Cheating the poor, robbing the poor, and coveting his meager property were condemned (Hosea 12:7; Micah 2:1-2). Amos denounced the abuse of the poor as follows:

Hear this, you who trample the needy, to do away with the humble of the land, saying,
"When will the new moon be over,
So that we may buy grain,
And the sabbath, that we may open the wheat market,
To make the bushel smaller and the shekel bigger,
And to cheat with dishonest scales,
So as to buy the helpless for money
And the needy for a pair of sandals,
And that we may sell the refuse of the wheat?"
The LORD has sworn by the pride of Jacob, "Indeed, I will never forget any of their deeds" (Amos 8:4-7).

Widows and orphans, people who might be especially oppressed, came under special protection of the law. "You shall not affict any widow or orphan. If you afflict him at all, and if he does cry out to Me, I will surely hear his cry" (Exodus 22:22-23). Taking a widow's garment in pledge was prohibited (Deuteronomy 24:17). When fields were reaped, all the forgotten sheaves were to be left for widows and orphans (Deuteronomy

44

24:19). Every third year the tithe of produce went to widows, orphans, and sojourners (Deuteronomy 26:12-13).

These regulations concerned the poor and oppressed of the theocracy. But the law also included rules for sojourners (Heb., *ger*). Israelites could not oppress them (Exodus 22:21; 23:9; Leviticus 19:33-34). Indeed, they were to love them (Deuteronomy 10:19). The gleanings of the vineyard and the harvest were to be left for them (Leviticus 19:10; 23:22; Deuteronomy 24:19-21). The protection of the cities of refuge was extended to them (Numbers 35:15; Joshua 20:9). They were ranked with widows and orphans as being defenseless (Psalm 94:6; Zechariah 7:10). As settlers they were virtually on the same level as Israelites (Leviticus 24:22) with a few exemptions: they were not included in the general liberation of slaves in the year of jubilee (Leviticus 25:45-46); they had no inheritance rights in the land, and they could not keep the Passover unless circumcised (Exodus 12:48).

A foreigner (Heb., *nokri*) was someone of another race and particularly another religion. Strict regulations were given against marrying strangers (Deuteronomy 7:1-6; 1 Kings 11:1-2). Interest could be taken from a *nokri* but not an Israelite (Deuteronomy 23:20). The protection afforded by Israelite laws benefited settlers for the most part, but not foreigners.

3. There were also many personal sins that had social implications. Swearing, lying, killing, stealing, and committing adultery brought sorrow to the people and eventually resulted in captivity (Hosea 4:2). Those sins were committed "because there is no faithfulness or kindness or knowledge of God in the land" (Hosea 4:1). Unjust leaders quite naturally influenced the lives of members of the theocracy (Micah 3:1-4).

45

Violations of God's marriage laws seriously disrupted family and social life. Divorce, rampant in the time of Malachi, had far-reaching consequences: it broke the pledge made at the time of marriage (Malachi 2:14), it violated God's original intention of one woman for one man (Malachi 2:15), it denied the rightful protection due the wife (2:16), and it clearly violated God's desire for man when He said, "I hate divorce" (2:16). During this same time, spiritually mixed marriages were being severely condemned by Nehemiah (13:23-27).

One cannot help but observe in passing that usually whenever Old Testament social ethics are made a norm for the church to follow and campaign for today, these teachings on divorce and mixed marriages are often conveniently deleted.

The contribution of theocratic ethics to us today. All the Bible is profitable. Whenever God gives a law to anybody at any time, it reveals something about His attitude toward the problem. This is true whether the law is binding forever on all people or temporarily on some. Thus whatever God required of His people Israel tells us something about God even if those specific commands are inapplicable to us today.

However, some of the guidelines are the same for both the theocracy and the church. Indeed, the outstanding feature of the Old Testament teaching (and when misunderstood, the outstanding error) is that the unit of society to which social ethics applied was the theocracy, the "in group," not outsiders. Similarly, the church's social responsibilities are primarily directed to the body. Many specifics of ethics under the theocracy are the same or similar to the specific commands given to the church. Concern for the poor, the orphan, and the widow are as much a New Testament theme as an Old Testament one.

46

Prohibitions against idolatry and personal sins with social ramifications are found in both the theocratic code and church law.

But some things are different. Members of the theocracy were not told to do good to all men. Members of the church are. Obedience to the theocratic government involved much more than obedience does today. Regulations concerning giving were different then from what they are now.

To sum up: the Old Testament focuses on concern for the oppressed within the theocracy. It does not command the establishment of justice in the world, nor the care of all the poor and oppressed in the world. It is more "isolationalist" than the New Testament. But it does show God's love for justice and holiness in personal living as well as in the group. It does show God's abiding hatred of sin.

Chapter Seven

Jesus' Teaching on Poverty and Wealth

Jesus' Teaching on Poverty and Wealth

From more than a dozen references to money in the teachings of our Lord, we glean some important principles to guide us in this very practical area of personal and social ethics.

On poverty. Four principles emerge from Christ's teachings concerning poverty.

1. Poverty is an inevitable social phenomenon. It was at Bethany that the Lord uttered the well-known statement: "For the poor you always have with you, and whenever you wish, you can do them good; but you do not always have Me" (Mark 14:7). The occasion was His anointing by Mary, the sister of Martha and Lazarus (John 12:3), with costly ointment of pure nard. These twelve ounces of highly aromatic perfume were

worth the equivalent of a year's wages for the average agricultural worker.

When the disciples protested that the money might better have been given to the poor, the Lord made His well-known remark. The statement should never be understood callously, as if Christ were saying one need never concern himself with the alleviation of poverty. Actually Christ was saying that opportunities always exist to do something for the poor, but not always to anoint Him as Mary did. Opportunities to anoint Him would soon vanish since He was about to be put to death, but opportunities to help the poor would always be present, since poor people would always be around. Or, to put it another way, on that particular occasion an extravagant gift of perfumed ointment was more appropriate than a donation to the poor.

2. The existence of poverty around us does not necessarily constitute a call to action to alleviate that poverty. If this were not a valid inference from this incident, then the ointment should have been sold and the proceeds given to the poor.

If the presence of poverty in this world constitutes a call to action to alleviate it, then no Christian could ever justify having anything but the barest necessities of life since the poor surround us in this ever-shrinking world. In view of the fact that ten thousand people die every day of starvation or malignant malnutrition, how could any Christian justify ever eating a steak when he could eat hamburger? Or how could anyone justify eating hamburger when he could eat cereal and send the money saved to the poor?

The necessity, or even the worth, of a good deed does not in and of itself determine whether I should do it. I must know the specific will of God at that time concerning doing or not doing that particular good work. Or, to be very explicit, it

52

may be the will of God to own and "waste" expensive perfume on some occasion rather than not to own it, or even sell it, and give the equivalent amount of money to the poor. Also it is equally true that the opposite course of action may be the will of God for another occasion.

3. The Lord commended sacrificial giving and condemned selfish and showy giving. The object of His commendation was a poverty-stricken widow who gave all she had (Mark 12:41-44). The Lord has just finished teaching in the Court of the Gentiles. Passing through one of the nine gates in the dividing wall around the temple proper, He walked into the Court of the Women where the treasury was. Throngs of people were casting their offerings into the thirteen trumpet-like receptacles placed there for receiving charitable contributions.

Just as He passed by, a destitute widow cast in two small coins, the least valuable of any denomination in use at that time, but coins that represented her entire means of sustenance. Her gift not only demonstrated the highest kind of sacrifice, but also showed her complete trust in God to sustain her and provide her with a means of earning more. There seem to be two principles exhibited here: first, all should give, even the poor; and second, people should give proportionately and generously. The test of true giving is not simply what is given but what is retained.

This is a very important example for all, especially those who feel that the poor are somehow exempt from giving and those who think that the rich are obliged only to give the same proportion as everyone else, rather than a greater proportion.

4. The Lord also taught although the poor are blessed, it is quite desirable to work for self-advancement. Luke's account of the Beatitudes

53

begins: "Blessed are you who are poor" (Luke 6:20). Undoubtedly actual poverty is meant here (in contrast to Matthew's record that directs the blessing to the "poor in spirit").

However, the Lord is not saying that the state of poverty is more desirable, as if men should renounce all their possessions. Elsewhere He clearly commends those who work for self-betterment. His parable of the pounds commends trading and legitimate gain (Luke 19:11-28). So does the parable of the talents (Matthew 25:14-30). And in both stories those who worked hard are allowed to enjoy the fruit of their labors. They were not expected to support the one who had done nothing with his pound or talent.

On wealth. We can also glean certain principles from our Lord's teaching concerning wealth.

1. He did *not* say that possessions were necessarily or intrinsically wrong. His circle of friends included well-to-do people like Joseph of Arimathaea (Matthew 27:57), Nicodemus (John 3:1), the centurion of Capernaum (Luke 7:2), the family of Lazarus, Mary, and Martha of Bethany (Luke 10:38), and the several women who contributed to His and the disciples' support from their private funds (Luke 8:3). None was condemned for possessing wealth nor expected to redistribute it evenly among fellow Jews. But each was expected to use his or her wealth properly, and we know from the Scriptures that some of them did.

What about the encounter with the rich young ruler (Matthew 19:16-22)? Does that incident teach that wealthy people should disperse their possessions? Not at all. The thrust of the dialogue is not about social responsibility or action but about sin and salvation. And actually the conversation never gets as far as salvation, for the young man was never willing to acknowledge his need of a Savior.

True, he approached the Lord asking about eternal life (v. 16), but Christ, knowing that he really did not sense any need to be saved by other than his own works, tried first to elicit a confession of sin from him. So the Lord asked him to measure himself against part of the Ten Commandments, and by his own confession he said he measured up perfectly. Then Jesus put him to another test—go and sell your possessions and give them to the poor. But since he was unwilling to do that, it proved that he in reality had not kept the commandments he claimed to have kept a moment before. Certainly his unwillingness to give to the poor shows that he did not love his neighbor as he loved himself.

At that point the man should have acknowledged that he was a sinner in need of something his own good works could not provide in order to be saved. The Lord did not say that to keep the law is to guarantee eternal life. He was showing that by not keeping the law the man was a sinner in need of a Savior. But his refusal to acknowledge that brought the conversation to an end.

2. The Lord did teach that riches make it more difficult for a man to enter the kingdom of God (Matthew 19:24). The needle referred to in this verse is a sewing needle that accentuates the solemnity of the warning. However, Christ did not say that a rich man could not be saved, but only that it is more difficult for him to be saved, since such a person seldom senses his personal need as readily as a poorer person does.

3. The Lord warned that a person's life does not consist in the abundance of his possessions (Luke 12:15). Abundance can be used to help others or it can feed one's own greed.

Christ had been approached by a man who

wanted Him to settle a dispute between him and his brother over an inheritance. The Lord refused. But He did take the opportunity to talk about greed, undoubtedly indicating that the man who asked Him for help did not come with pure motives. The land of a gentleman farmer produced an abundance of crops, so much so that the landowner was embarrassed by his riches and did not know what to do. Apparently he could not use all the abundance himself, so his options were either to store it or to share it. The latter option he never thought of. But in choosing to build more storehouses he made several false assumptions: that he would be satisfied with more, and that he would live to enjoy what he had stored. But he did not live to enjoy even the next day after making the decision. And the Lord's point was that what a person has should be used for God's glory rather than for personal greed (v. 21).

4. The Lord did instruct His followers on the use of money in the service of others in the parable of the unjust steward (Luke 16:1-13). The ingenuity of the dishonest manager in using his opportunity to secure his own future was commended by Christ for consideration, not for following the example of dishonesty.

When the manager was caught in his dishonesty and knew he would be fired, he contacted two of his boss's debtors and discounted their bills. That ingratiated him with those who owed the payments, and it also recovered for his boss at least part of the debts. And it helped secure his future, for after he was fired he expected return favors from those he had helped.

The Lord recommends that His followers be as ingenious in using money, "the mammon of unrighteousness," to assure rewards in heaven (v. 9). The point is clear: use money wisely in this life, so that when it fails (that is, so that when you can no longer use money because death has occurred), they (those you have helped during your lifetime) may receive (that is, welcome) you into heaven. These are believers helping other believers (or at least people who become believers), for both donors and donees in this story are seen in "everlasting habitations." Faith alone opens heaven, but good works gain an abundant entrance into heaven with rewards. Use money then to help others who follow Christ. No clear word is found here concerning the believer's responsibility outside the circle of disciples (except to evangelize). This is a story about doing good to those of the household of faith rather than to all men.

Summary. Some conclusions and observations can be drawn from these principles and teachings of our Lord concerning poverty and wealth.

1. His chief emphasis was on the proper use of money, both for those who may have a lot and for those who have little. Having money or lacking it is not in itself wrong, but how a person uses whatever he has is the important matter. All should be generous.

2. The focus of proper use of money is the circle of God's people. Christ did not give directions in these passages about social responsibilities beyond the community of His followers. He certainly promoted no program for the elimination of poverty or the equalization of wealth.

Chapter Eight

Jesus' Teaching Concerning Duties to All People

Jesus' Teaching Concerning Duties to All People

In His teachings concerning poverty and wealth the Lord did not expand on His followers' responsibilities beyond the circle of the community of disciples. But are there no universals in the Lord's teachings? Does He not commend social service toward all men? Has the believer no obligation to unbelievers other than preaching the gospel to them? Other aspects of His teachings do bear upon these questions and furnish guidelines for biblical answers.

Be salt and light. "You are the salt of the earth. . . . You are the light of the world" (Matthew 5:13-14). Here in this familiar saying Christ does relate His followers in some way to the whole world. But in precisely what way? Let us examine these metaphors separately.

What was Christ's intention in likening believers to salt? Usually it is understood to mean that believers are to be a preservative force in this world. Certainly this is a basic part of the concept. But how are believers to do this? By being salt that is untainted and uncontaminated.

Good salt preserves. Salt also gives flavor. Salt cleanses. Salt de-ices. Salt creates thirst. And salt, when poured into a wound, stings. But only good salt does any of these things.

The Lord issues two warnings to believers who would be this kind of force in a corrupt world. First, they must expect persecution. The world does not stand with open arms to welcome Christian salt. Rather, it will, as Israel of old did to her prophets, often persecute those who try to stem the tide of evil. But that only happens to good salt. Second, the Lord warned that if the salt itself gets contaminated then it will be of no use to do what it was designed to do. Plummer summarized well when he wrote: "Perhaps the connecting thought is, that Christians, like the Prophets who saved Israel from corruption, must be ready to suffer persecution. . . . But they must beware lest, instead of preserving others, they themselves become tainted with rottenness. The salt *must* be in close contact with that which it preserves; and too often, while Christians raise the morality of the world, they allow their own morality to be lowered by the world" (Alfred Plummer, *An Exegetical Commentary of the Gospel According to S. Matthew* [London: Robert Scott, 1911], p. 72). Salt means preserve; preserve yourself first in purity, and then preserve everything you touch in purity.

But salt has a second significance from its use in the Old Testament. Salt was a symbol of that which gave life and permanency to a covenant.

62

That is the meaning behind the Old Testament expression "a covenant of salt" (Numbers 18:19; 2 Chronicles 13:5). Eating salt with another person signified that the two were bound together in loyalty (Ezra 4:14, RSV*). A covenant of salt was a permanent, living agreement. Elisha purified the spring at Jericho with salt in order that there would "not be from there death or unfruitfulness [lit., miscarriage] any longer" (2 Kings 2:21).

To be salt in this world means to give life, preserving influence, stability, and holiness to this world. And the response of the world to good salt is apt to be persecution and rejection.

The metaphor of light acts as a safeguard lest believers think they have light in themselves with which to enlighten the world. We are reflections of Him who is the light of the world (John 8:12). Light both attracts and repels. The believer's life and testimony concerning the One who is the light of the world will attract some and repel others (2 Corinthians 2:16). Our light should be conspicuous (set on a hill) and consistent (giving light to the house). It should be displayed in public (on a hill) and in private (in the house). But most of all light should be seen and that by means of the believer's good works. In this way the Father is glorified.

> Cowards can always find plausible excuses for the policy of obscuration—reasons of prudence and wisdom: gradual accustoming of men to new ideas; deference to the prejudices of good men; avoidance of rupture by premature outspokenness; but generally the true reason is fear of unpleasant consequences to oneself. Their conduct Jesus represents as disloyalty to God. . . . The temptation arises from the fact—a stern law of the moral world it is—that

* *Revised Standard Version.*

just when most glory is likely to accrue to God, least glory comes to the light-bearer; not glory but dishonour and evil treatment [are] his share. Many are ready enough to let their light shine when honour comes to themselves. But *their* "light" is not true heaven-kindled light. . . . [A. B. Bruce, "The Synoptic Gospels," *The Expositor's Greek Testament* (Grand Rapids: Eerdmans, n.d.), 1:103]

Thus the believer's character and works affect the world by giving life, preserving, attracting and repelling, and glorifying the Father.

Be loving to your neighbor. No discussion of Jesus' teaching would be complete without including a study of the parable of the good Samaritan (Luke 10:25-37). Scribes in Israel were interpreters, teachers, and judges of the law. The scribe who evoked the story of the good Samaritan came to the Lord to tempt Him. His question was simple, basic, and to the point: What must I do to inherit eternal life? Because at that time men were still living under the law, the Lord asked him what the law demanded. The scribe's answer was again simple, basic, and to the point. He quoted the two greatest commandments. In response, the Lord said that if he would continue to do these he would live. But, of course, neither this man nor any other could love the Lord with all his heart and his neighbor as himself. So in order to justify his inability to keep these basic commandments, the scribe seized on the one word in the commandments that was ambiguous, the one word on which an argument could be raised. Playing to the grandstand, he asked for a definition of the word *neighbor.*

Then followed the story of the Good Samaritan. Who is my neighbor according to this story? He is the person in need who crosses my path. The man who was robbed was the Samaritan's neighbor, and the Samaritan obviously loved him as himself. But the Samaritan was also in need of concern, and he in turn was the neighbor of the Jewish scribe. Of course, the scribe refused to accept that fact. Since he would not recognize the Samaritan as his neighbor (Samaritans were considered scum), he could not claim to have fulfilled the law. Rather, he needed to acknowledge his sin and cast himself on the mercy of God.

The parable also clearly extols good works done to those in need who cross our path. That may involve someone of different economic status, different race, different religion, or different political persuasion.

That much is clear. What is complicated, however, is how to do something about the needs of the literally millions of people who cross our path by means of television. To do something for one robbed man on the Jericho road is one thing; to do something for thousands and millions of starved and oppressed people in many countries of this world is another thing. What can the believer do who is sensitive to the needs of so many neighbors? Best he should start with those neighbors closest to him—in his church, in his circle of acquaintances, in his town. Our Lord went about doing good (Acts 10:38) to those in Palestine whose paths crossed His, but not even to everyone in that small land, and certainly not to anyone in Philippi, or Antioch, or Rome. Today we can extend our good works into a wider geographical area than Christ did because of communication, cooperative agencies, and so on. But we should never overlook those closest to us. God will have to guide each one in this matter, for no one, nor all of us together, could meet the needs that so many neighbors have.

Matthew 25:31-46. Undoubtedly this future

65

judgment scene is one of the most often used passages in support of the idea that Christians are primarily responsible to feed and clothe the world. The interpretation of the "brethren" in verse 40 is crucial. Harry Emerson Fosdick wrote that Jesus "even said that at the judgment seat . . . human service to hungry, thirsty, naked, sick, and imprisoned would prove the one passport to the favor of the Eternal" (*Adventurous Religion and Other Essays* [New York: Association, 1926], p. 37). An evangelical defines "brethren" this way: "The 'brethren' referred to here include all members of the human race, not solely those who are brothers in the added sense of being born again" (David O. Moberg, *Inasmuch* [Grand Rapids: Eerdmans, 1965], p. 39).

According to all rapture schemes that event will have already taken place by the time this judgment occurs, so the church will be with the King. Now if the church is with the King and Gentiles are before the King, the brethren must be the only remaining group, the Jews, Christ's natural brethren (see Romans 9:3). In the days of tribulation and apostasy that will precede this judgment, to render service to a persecuted Jew by feeding, clothing, or visiting him will be done at the risk of one's own life and will be the most conclusive evidence of one's own spiritual relationship to the Lord. Although the passage does not teach that all men everywhere are my social responsibility, it does teach that redeemed people of that future day will show to the world the grace of God by their good and daring works to "the brethren."

Although this is the precise meaning of the passage, it can also certainly be applied to remind God's people at any time in history that feeding, clothing, and visiting those who are being persecuted are good works that glorify God (see James 1:27 and 2:15-16).

Summary. In relation to all people, the Lord taught that His followers are to be untainted salt, public and private reflections of Himself, and Spirit-led helpers of various neighbors. That behavior demands purity of life, boldness of witness, and sensitivity to needs.

Chapter Nine

The Priorities
of Our Lord

The Priorities
of Our Lord

Many needs of many people confronted the Lord just as they do us. But He did not meet them all. What can we learn from His life and ministry that will help give us a sense of discernment and scale of priorities?

Physical or spiritual? No one can help every other person in the world. Even our Lord did not help everyone He contacted, nor did He command His followers to do so.

It is perfectly obvious that He did not heal everyone who needed it. In the thirty-five recorded miracles of Christ performed on specific individuals or groups there are thirty-nine cases of healing. Of those, two (Malchus and the Syrophoenician's daughter) involved individuals outside the commonwealth of Israel. Although He healed an unspecified number on several occasions, there were many others who crossed His path whom He did not heal. We know, for example, that a multitude of sick, blind, lame, and withered people were gathered at the pool of Bethesda (John 5:3); yet Christ threaded His way through the crowd to find a single individual to heal—a man who, oddly enough, exhibited no faith that he could be healed. Our Lord could just as easily have healed two, ten, or a hundred more that same day, but He only healed one. If need always carries with it a responsibility to respond, then our Lord furnishes no example of this in His ministry of physical healing.

Neither did the Lord feed all those who were hungry. On two occasions He fed over ten thousand people—but only a single meal. He did not continue to supply them with food, though some of them likely had a genuine need of food later. Furthermore, the healings and feedings were not done primarily to benefit those who were healed and fed, but to glorify God, or to teach the disciples, or to confirm His claims to be God. The physical benefits seemed secondary to the spiritual lessons intended to be learned. The Lord's priorities were spiritual.

Some would charge that this emphasis on the spiritual over the physical is a false dualism that cannot be supported by biblical teaching on the nature of man. If we would properly stress the unity of man, then, it is said, we would erase the false distinction between winning "souls" versus feeding "bodies." But not only would it erase the distinction, but it would also logically lead to incorporating social action as an equal part of the gospel message.

Unquestionably man is a unitary being, but Scripture views man as a being of great complex-

72

ity and varied functioning (see 1 Corinthians 14:14-15; Romans 7:22-23; 2 Corinthians 5:1-5, 8 that distinguish various aspects of man's being). Although he is a unitary being he has a corporeal aspect and an incorporeal aspect. Body and spirit are distinguished in the Bible (James 2:26); one can minister in the realm of the spirit (1 Corinthians 2:11; 14:14) and one can minister in the realm of the physical (James 2:16). Thus to be fully biblical one must recognize both the unitary nature of man and the distinct complexities within that unit. Our ministry may be directed toward any or all of those aspects of man's being, but the ministry may vary in intensity or direction according to situations and circumstances.

Back to our Lord's example. While He did attend to physical and material needs on occasion, He gave first priority to spiritual needs. The angel announced Him to Joseph as the one who "will save His people from their sins" (Matthew 1:21). John the Baptist designated Him as the "Lamb of God who takes away the sin of the world" (John 1:29), and He Himself declared that He came "to seek and to save that which was lost" (Luke 19:10). He also came to serve, to teach, to set an example, to show God's love, but above all, He came, as His primary purpose, to save.

Justice or subservience? In the twentieth century social involvement in many countries has been in the political arena. That is not necessarily wrong, but at this point we are only examining the example of the Lord in this regard.

Clearly, Jesus did not attempt to reform the Roman government under which He lived. He acknowledged the rule of Rome (Matthew 22:21). When faced with the question of paying the poll tax that was due annually and that went directly to Caesar in Rome, our Lord did not address the more basic question of whether or not Rome had

73

the right to occupy Palestine. If not, then should the Jewish people try to gain independence from Romè? They were an oppressed people, yet the Lord did not suggest any action to free them from that subservience. He simply said that if one accepts the benefits of government (in that instance by using the money Rome coined), then one is obligated to pay taxes.

The particular denarius with which the poll tax was paid bore the image of the emperor and acclaimed him to be God. The inscription on the coin read: "Tiberius Caesar Augustus, son of the Divine Augustus." Yet our Lord did not address the question of idolatry that some of the people believed was involved in simply using these coins. He simply said, "Pay."

But on that occasion the Lord also said something else that gave an indication of His scale of priorities. He reminded His hearers that they had an obligation to God when He said that they should render to God the things that are God's. He was making a connection between the image of Caesar stamped on the denarius and the image of God stamped on every person. The point was clear: the Jews were subjects of Caesar. His image was stamped on the coin. What then did they owe Caesar? The tax. We are men, and as members of the human race we bear the stamp of the image of God. What then do we owe God? Ourselves. The more important priority is not our relation to the government under which we live, but our relation to God. Once again His priorities were spiritual. You can afford to be without political justice, but you cannot afford to refuse to be subservient to God. Our Lord was not a political revolutionary; but He certainly was a radical religious revolutionary.

On another occasion the Lord was asked to settle a dispute between two brothers (Luke

74

12:13-21). He refused to do so because He would not usurp the sphere of constituted authority. The manner with which He addressed the questioner was severe and shows Jesus' indignation at being asked to step out of His sphere of ministry ("man" in v. 14). However, the Lord did not leave the matter there. He used the request as an occasion for a sermon on coveteousness and the priority of soul over substance (v. 20). Once again He gave priority to the spiritual rather than the material or political.

Rights or ministry? The incident concerning payment of the Temple tax also reveals Jesus' priorities (Matthew 17:24-27). The tax was based on the regulation of Exodus 30:11-16 and was collected from every male Jew twenty or over, including those living in foreign countries. It was used to keep the Temple in Jerusalem in good repair.

Seeking out Peter, the tax collectors asked him if Jesus would pay the tax. Peter responded quickly and affirmatively, but then had second thoughts. Anticipating Peter's misgivings, the Lord questioned Peter and instructed him in the uniqueness of His person. There followed a short dialogue that led to the conclusion that Jesus, as the owner of the Temple (because He is God, Malachi 3:1), was exempt from paying the tax. Jesus clearly claimed exemption because He is God. Nevertheless, through a miracle of finding a coin in a fish's mouth, the taxes for Peter and the Lord were paid.

However, it is the reason why Christ paid that is instructive—"lest we give them offense" (Matthew 17:27). The same verb is used in Romans 14:21 and 1 Corinthians 8:13 to teach that Christians should sometimes surrender their freedom for the sake of others. Here the Lord demonstrated a principle all reformers could follow;

namely, "the avoidance of actions which are not absolutely essential for the success of the reform, and which, because easily misunderstood, and so arousing prejudice, would make it more difficult for others to join in the good movement. . . . Some who might otherwise have listened to Him would have turned away had He seemed by His example to teach that the Temple-services were not worth maintaining" (Alfred Plummer, *A Critical Commentary on the Gospel According to Matthew* [London: Scott, 1911], p. 246).

On other occasions our Lord cleansed the Temple of the money changers and predicted the destruction of the Temple. But here He conformed to a temple law not even commanded in the Old Testament. Not offending for the sake of ministry took priority over insisting on His rights.

Summary. These examples clearly demonstrate that the Lord gave top priority to spiritual needs. Though not insensitive to physical needs, He met relatively few of them. Though always obedient to government, He led no attempt to reform the system or correct injustices. He always kept His principal purpose for being on earth in sharp focus.

And His commission to us follows the same priorities.

Chapter Ten

The Christian and His Civic Responsibilities

The Christian and His Civic Responsibilities

The dual citizenship of the believer that the Lord affirmed (Matthew 22:21) is reiterated by the apostle Paul. While a citizen of heaven (Philippians 3:20), Paul nonetheless enjoyed and used the privileges of his Roman citizenship on several occasions (Acts 22:25 ff.; 25:10-12).

Without question, *obedience* is the key word the apostles use to describe the Christian's responsibility to civil government. In the classic passage, Romans 13:1-7, Paul commands obedience and submission for several reasons: because governmental authority is ordained of God (v. 1); because resistance to government is, in the final analysis, resistance to God (v. 2); because government generally opposes evil (v. 4);

and because our conscience tells us to obey (v. 5).

Eight or nine years and several imprisonments later, during which time Paul had ample opportunity to rethink his position, he nevertheless gave the same advice: "Remind them to be subject to rulers" (Titus 3:1). Mistreatment at the hands of the Roman government was not sufficient existential grounds for changing his mind.

About the same time Paul wrote to Titus, Peter wrote to people in various parts of the empire that they should submit for the following reasons: submission shows our obedience to God (1 Peter 2:13); it is the will of God (v. 15); it is a good testimony to the unsaved (v. 15).

Both Peter and Paul wrote under the reign of Nero (A.D. 54-68). Romans was written when Nero's government was good, but when Peter wrote, Nero's persecution of Christians had likely begun. If Peter was in Rome when he wrote 1 Peter (that seems likely from 1 Peter 5:13), this makes what he said even more striking.

Notice too that the voice of the verb *be subject* in both Romans and Titus indicates that obedience is to be given freely of the believer's own accord.

To what extent should a Christian obey? None of the passages cited offers any exceptions or special cases that would call for disobedience. However, two New Testament examples of disobedience are instructive. One comes from Peter's well-known statement: "We must obey God rather than men" (Acts 5:29), a statement regarding disobeying the command of the Sanhedrin that had not only religious power but wide political power at that time. The Sanhedrin's command clearly contradicted a command of God thus requiring disobedience, though not exempting the believers from punishment.

The second example ilustrates pressure that

can properly be applied to bring governmental authorities to do what they are supposed to do. The incident occurred at Philippi where Paul staged a first-century sit-in. Having been beaten without a trial, he refused to move until the authorities came and apologized for violating his rights as a Roman citizen (Acts 16:37). He used a legitimate tactic to compel the Roman authorities to fulfill their lawful responsibilities.

In addition to obeying governments, Christians are, second, to respect authorities (1 Peter 2:17). To all men we must give honor; to other believers, love; to God, fear; and to the King, constant honor (the tense in this last command changes to the present).

Obedience, respect, and, third, support for government (Romans 13:6-7; compare Matthew 22:21). Paul's teaching parallels Christ's—that is, since we receive benefits from government we must support government.

Fourth, we must pray for rulers (1 Timothy 2:1-2). Our prayers should include thanksgiving for rulers (often difficult to do) and should include all in authority, not simply rulers who agree with us.

Those responsibilities are clear, but they do not include revolution even when rulers were anti-God. The believer's heavenly citizenship is far more important, for his earthly sojourn is temporary. Another has summarized well.

The early Christians were subject to a power which required them to do that which was forbidden by their religion. To that extent and within those limits they could not and did not obey it; but they never encouraged in any way resistance or rebellion. . . . He only disobeyed when it was necessary to do so for conscience sake. The point of importance is the detach-

81

ment of the two spheres of activity. The Church and the State are looked upon as different bodies, each with a different work to perform. To designate this or that form of government as 'Christian,' and support it on these grounds, would have been quite alien to the whole spirit of those days. The Church must influence the world by its hold on the hearts and consciences of individuals. . . . [William Sanday and Arthur C. Headlam, *The Epistle to the Romans* (New York: Scribner's, 1895), p. 372]

Liberation theology, prominent in so many countries, directly counters this New Testament teaching on civic responsibilities. Casting Marxism in Christian terminology, this viewpoint advocates the overthrow of oppressive governments and economic systems. The poor and oppressed of the earth, God's true people, must be liberated at any cost. Thus violence plays a vital and necessary role in liberation theology.

Furthermore, this violence is not immoral. Indeed, it is commended. "A supreme sense of moral worth pervades the subversive enterprise in Latin America" (Denis Goulet, *A New Moral Order: Studies in Development Ethics and Liberation Theology* [Maryknoll, New York: Orbis, 1974], p. 63). "Man is absolved from inhumanity and brutality in the present, as the time of transition, the time which does not count" (Rubem A. Alves, *A Theology of Human Hope* [Washington, D.C.: Corpus, 1969], p. 155). Obviously in liberation theology salvation is through politics, but a breed of political action that seeks the overthrow of governments, not obedient living under them. Liberation theology's response to the teaching of Romans 13 is that this passage "is a highly arbitrary Biblical norm; Romans 13 must at least be considered in tandem with Revelation 13, which describes the state as 'the beast' " (Robert McAfee Brown, *Theology in a New Key* [Philadelphia: Westminster, 1978], p. 106). The beast, of course, is a person who, to be sure, will head a government that will persecute believers. Nevertheless the perverted use of power does not invalidate the fact that the powers that be are still ordained of God. Liberation theology is not a New Testament theology.

Christians may be called upon to live under governments that are incompatible or even opposed to Christianity. But there is no biblical mandate to overthrow such governments or to Christianize them. Some, however, believe that Christianizing is God's purpose today. Since the risen Christ is Lord, we should expect that His lordship will be effected in all areas of life today, including the political. This is a form of postmillennialism, often promoted by those of the Reformed tradition who would normally be expected to be amillennial. The principal errors of this teaching are two: it fails to recognize that the theocratic laws of the Old Testament are not the laws of the New Testament; and it roots its teaching about politics in the doctrine of Christ (i.e., since He is Lord, that lordship ought to govern governments).

Observe: liberation theology sees governments as instruments of salvation; Christianizers see them as instruments of lordship; but the Bible sees them as gifts of God's providence.

What place do movements have that attempt to promote righteousness in government while recognizing the need for obedience and the distinction between the New Testament teaching and the Old Testament theocracy? It is universally true that "righteousness exalts a nation, but sin is a disgrace to any people" (Proverbs 14:34). But no nation except Israel can claim that God will

83

heal their land if the people humble themselves and pray (2 Chronicles 7:14). Can you imagine offering that promise today to an underground church in a country ruled by an atheistic government? The promise was not given nor can it be offered to just any country anywhere, anytime.

Nevertheless, promoting righteousness is a worthy activity for any Christian, including promoting it in the political arena. It should be done first of all by prayer, for it is God who raises up and removes rulers. It should be done by personal holy living in all our relation to governments. It may also involve concerted group action. If the government permits open and free assembly, grants a free vote, or offers avenues of legal protest, there is no reason why these means should not be used by Christians. In fact, there is every good reason why they should be used. Though having Christian officials cannot guarantee righteousness or even uniformity of viewpoint on issues, if the Christian is maturing in the faith and qualified and competent in his field he should have a different perspective and lifestyle and be a better civil servant. The priority each individual believer can give to such concerted action will vary depending on his calling in life. No New Testament mandate ever gives it top priority.

The Christian's primary responsibilities are evangelism and godly living. Through witnessing he changes people; through godly living he does affect society; and through private and public obedience he honors God.

Chapter Eleven

The Christian
and Poverty

The Christian and Poverty

Money is one of God's great gifts of providence to people. In the Bible as a whole, wealth is regarded as evil only if it is improperly accumulated or used. We are given money as one of God's gifts to use as a stewardship from Him. All that we have, including material possessions, comes from His good hand (1 Corinthians 4:7) and should be used for His glory.

But many questions face the earnest believer who wants to use his money for the glory of God. What is the proper place for planning, saving, investing? How much should one give? What are good priorities to follow in trying to meet the many demands on one's giving? How can one sincerely face questions like worldwide famine and poverty?

Although the New Testament does not give individualized answers to all these questions, it does give principles to guide the Christian in the proper use of money in the different seasons of life and in every economic stratum of society.

Possessions. Having money and lacking it can both be in the will of God. The Bible regards wealth as evil only if improperly used. It is the love of money that is the root of all evil (1 Timothy 6:10). Further, the rich are never told to give all their wealth away, but to be generous, not to trust in possessions, and to enjoy what God gives (1 Timothy 6:17-19). Ananias and Sapphira were judged not because they refused to give all their possessions to the church, but because they pretended to give all away when in reality they did not (Acts 5:1-11). Their sin was not wealth, but hypocrisy. And Peter made it quite clear that their property was theirs, both before and, that which was left, after the sale.

Paul experienced both conditions of having and lacking possessions (Philippians 4:12). He was not more in the Lord's will in one condition or the other (compare James 1:9-10). Contentment is the important lesson to learn in whatever state. For the person who has plenty it is much easier to be content, but he must constantly be on guard against money becoming an idol. The one who has little must also learn contentment, though that does not mean he must abandon legitimate means of self-advancement.

A person may also be rich or poor out of the will of God. Ill-gotten wealth will have to be accounted for in the day of judgment (James 5:3, 9). If poverty results from laziness or lack of discipline and management, then others are under no obligation to support those who are poor for those reasons. Paul commanded that if a man did not wish to work he should not eat (2 Thessalonians 3:10). Neither the individual believer nor the church has any responsibility to support such people.

Planning. Planning for the future is prudent, and the New Testament details three relationships in which this should be done. First, in relation to widowed parents or grandparents (1 Timothy 5:3-16), believers bear the primary responsibility for the aged in their families. The word *provide* in verse 8 means to think ahead and prepare for foreseeable needs. If there is no family to take the responsibility then the church assumes it. When that happens two additional principles operate: give temporary relief to younger widows (who are encouraged to remarry), and promise sustained support for older enrolled widows.

Second, in relation to parents' providing for their children (2 Corinthians 12:14), the principle is clear: Parents ought to save up for their children. But the difficult question is, how much is necessary and proper to obey this principle? The answer may be different in each family but may very well involve planning and forethought.

Third, in relation to caring for orphans (James 1:27)—how to do this is not stated, but if individual families act as guardians for an orphan, that would necessitate planning.

Prudent planning may involve investing. But the Christian who invests must ask regularly, when is enough enough? And yet he must not let capital lie idle, for that does not exercise responsible stewardship. As God may prosper him, he will decide that he has enough for himself and/or his children and then turn his acumen to supplying the needs of others. The practical problem is that most find it difficult to decide that there is enough for one's own needs. As prosperity increases, the standard of living usually does too. And that may not necessarily be outside the will of God up to a certain point. But surely there comes a certain point for some believers beyond which they need not go in improving their lifestyle. What that point is is a matter between the individual and God. What will be right for one may not be for another.

I think a believer should also try to answer the question, what is the social value of his investment? To do this fully is almost always impossible, but an attempt should be made to forecast an answer. Savings, stocks, bonds, land, and collectibles are all forms of investment that produce some sort of yield. Any investment should be examined not only as to its worthwhileness and honesty but also as to its social implications. Will it provide capital for the company that manages it to inject into society things that are harmful and contrary to morality? No investment can be totally guarded from misuse by those who manage it, but how could a believer knowingly invest in that which weakens the fabric of society?

In addition, I believe a Christian should not assume that capital should never be given away. At certain seasons of life it may be God's will to do so, and one must be open and sensitive to that possibility.

Giving. Giving is the proof of love (1 John 3:17). Giving to others flows from a heart of love, and the apostles, building on this truth, give clear guidelines for Spirit-led giving.

First, the individual should make regular provision for giving. Stewardship of one's personal assets should be systematically accounted for, so that funds are regularly available for giving (1 Corinthians 16:2). This laying aside should not be on the basis of an emotional plea, but on the basis of thoughtful, regular consideration based on a proper evaluation of God's prospering him. Provision for giving should be a part of a regular budget (2 Corinthians 8:12). It does not concern trusting God for what you do not have, but that of God trusting you to plan carefully with what you do have.

Second, our primary responsibility in the use of money is to care for the material needs of other believers (Galatians 6:10). From the beginning the New Testament church did this (Acts 2:44-45; 4:34-35). The right of holding private property was not abolished (4:34); community control was only assumed when goods or money was voluntarily given. Apparently this communal sharing was done temporarily (and only in Jerusalem) to meet the need created by the thousands of pilgrims whose stay in Jerusalem had been unexpectedly prolonged by their life-changing encounter with Christianity. Many stayed on to be taught and soon ran out of money, so the church stepped in to meet this need.

Later a large group of widows who turned to Christ found their support from a temple fund cut off. Again the church stepped in to undertake for her own.

Later, famine relief money was sent by the Christians in Antioch to those in Judea (Acts 11:27-30). And still later Paul led in taking a collection from the churches of Macedonia and Achaia for the poor saints in Jerusalem (Romans 15:25, 27; 2 Corinthians 8-9). This relief extended over a period of time (2 Corinthians 9:2) and involved organized and cooperative efforts (2 Corinthians 8:18-22). The money did not pass directly from donors to recipients but was cared for by a committee and then apparently distributed under the direction of the leaders of the church.

A fifth example comes from the gifts that were given to Paul and his associates for their missionary work. Apparently the Philippian church gave to Paul on at least three occasions (Philippians 4:16), and Paul rigorously defended the right of those engaged in the work to be supported by others (1 Corinthians 9:4-14).

All of these examples involved cooperative effort of a number of individuals working together to meet needs. Thus there is no justification for setting up a rigid division between personal and group responsibility in giving. Ultimately, of course, giving is an individual matter, but often the channel must involve a group.

Priorities in giving. No one can give to everything or even begin to meet fully needs around him. Here are some suggested guidelines that may help establish priorities for helping others.

1. Priorities as to people. It seems that we can glean some priorities as to those who should receive financial help: first, the Lord's servants, then the Lord's people who are in need, and then others. Those who minister spiritually to others have a right to expect to be supported by those who receive their ministry (1 Corinthians 9:11). Surely this is a primary responsibility of God's people. Galatians 6:10 establishes the other priorities: "So then, while we have opportunity, let us do good to all men, and especially to those who are of the household of the faith." Needy believers take priority over unbelievers.

2. Priority as to geography. However wide it may ultimately stretch, one's circle of concern must surely start with those among whom he lives. The needy in one's local church are the primary responsibility of the members of that church. As they are cared for, a person's charity can extend beyond the local group, but it will probably follow the knowledge a person has of needs elsewhere. The church's own missionaries

and the countries they serve will claim special interest. But again no single member can support the needs and interests of a local church; so the individual will give what he can and will have to trust the leaders of the group to distribute his and others' gifts properly.

3. Priority as to opportunity. "While we have opportunity," Paul wrote (Galatians 6:10). In verse 9 he has said that there is a season for reaping, and using the same word, season or opportunity, in verse 10 he says there is a season for doing good. And that season is when you have money to give and knowledge of needs to be met. So seize the opportunities as they present themselves.

Elsewhere Paul reminds us that the time (or season, again using the same word) is short (1 Corinthians 7:29), so do not delay to make the most of the resources and opportunities that you have, remembering that the totality of life is short at best. "All of us must live as loose to money and possessions as if we were actually giving them away. . . . All of us must keep on trying to find fresh ways of giving away more if possible year by year" (A.N. Trinton, *Whose World?* [London: Inter-Varsity, 1970], p. 175).

Chapter Twelve

The Christian and His Work

The Christian
and His Work

Work is a large part of almost everyone's life and provides opportunities often overlooked for responsible witness.

Before he sinned God gave Adam work to do (Genesis 1:28; 2:15), but after he sinned the element of toil became an inevitable part of man's attempts to make the earth provide for him (Genesis 3:17-19). Before the Fall the first man was told to subdue the earth (Genesis 1:28). After the Fall and after the Flood that specific command is significantly omitted from commands God gave to man (Genesis 9:1). Not until the future millennial kingdom will man regain his lost dominion over the earth (Hebrews 2:5-8).

God Himself is a working God. Our Lord worked

as a carpenter. All who are physically able are commanded to work if they want to eat (2 Thessalonians 3:10). Work is ordained of God.

What should be the believer's attitude toward his status in the social structure, and how can the believer use his work to further the gospel?

Attitude toward work. A proper attitude toward work involves both a sense of calling and a sense of contentment (1 Corinthians 7:17-24). The calling referred to seven times in these verses includes both the calling to be a Christian and the calling to a particular station or activity in life. Wherever he is in life and whatever he is called to do, the believer is "with God" (v. 24). Assuming that he is not in any immoral activity, the believer can be assured that God's calling makes any secular or religious work a work with God.

A believer should also have a sense of contentment. Let him walk in that calling (v. 17), let him remain in that calling (v. 20), let him remain (v. 24), the apostle reiterates. Paul does not mean that a person may never change jobs. Verse 21 means that if a slave has a chance to gain his freedom he should take it. Throughout, Paul's emphasis is on serving the Lord in the conditions of life to which we are called.

Use of work. Paul did not advocate any kind of revolutionary actions against the structures of life and employment. Normal Christian conduct and witness by the believer are the forces that will effect change. Proper conduct on the part of slaves (and thus employees) means obedience, reverence, sincerity, wholehearted work, and no wrong doing (Ephesians 6:5-8; Colossians 3:22-25). On the part of masters (and thus employers) it means no threats, fair pay, and honest dealings (Ephesians 6:9; Colossians 4:1; James 5:4).

Those instructions rule out for workers sloppy work, "slowdowns," featherbedding, and

98

demands for higher wages simply because others are getting them. For employers they outlaw corporate pressure tactics, unfair or unkind treatment of employees, and all dishonest practices (even though they may be "acceptable business practices"). They do not outlaw union activities any more than they forbid corporate activities.

> The Christian worker, however, even on the assembly line, can find a sense of ultimate purpose and meaning unknown to the unbeliever. While modern industry, at worst, may distort and thwart one's spiritual sonship during work hours, it cannot really make a machine of one who is a son of God. . . . The 340 permanent staff members of Mayo Clinic are not less helpful to mankind because each individual is a specialist. . . . It is equally possible, and imperative, for the specialist with a sense of calling and mission to think of each person as "my private patient, to be handled as if he were the only patient I have." Someone will say that this high response is more natural to the worker who deals directly with the persons who benefit from his labors, and this is true enough. But no worker's responsibility is lessened simply because he serves an invisible neighbor. Many a life has been saved by a properly tightened screw, and many lost through an improperly tightened bolt. [Carl F. H. Henry, *Aspects of Christian Social Ethics* (Grand Rapids: Eerdmans, 1964), pp. 59-60.]

Summary. In matters related to employment, change is effected by each Christian fulfilling his responsibility to act with honesty and fairness in his respective position. Nowhere does the Bible call upon Christians to organize a campaign to effect corporate changes in, say, General Chariots Corporation. But it does call on Christians in the

United Chariot Workers Union and Christians in the management of General Chariots Corporation to work and act like Christians.

The New Testament perspective on a believer's work life is seen in two verses: "Whatever you do, do your work heartily, as for the Lord rather than for men; knowing that from the Lord you will receive the reward of the inheritance. It is the Lord Christ whom you serve" (Colossians 3:23-24).

Chapter Thirteen

No Distinction

No Distinction

One of the great distinctives of this age is that "there is no distinction" (Romans 3:22). In a real sense, the principle of impartiality summarizes the perspective of the New Testament in several important areas.

In disseminating the gospel. This is the message of Romans 3: all have sinned without distinction and all may believe without distinction. Today it is no longer necessary to be an Israelite or a proselyte to Judaism to have acceptance with God, but all may believe, regardless of race or religion.

That was the great lesson Peter was taught in Acts 10. As he was praying he fell into a trance and saw a great sheet full of all sorts of ceremonially unclean animals being let down from heaven, animals he as a Jew was forbidden to eat. Suddenly a voice commanded Peter to kill and eat them. Peter refused, even though God assured him that He had cleansed those animals, and the action was repeated three times. But Peter did respond to the command to accompany three men to the house of Cornelius. Two days later they arrived there, all the time Peter pondering the significance of the vision.

Obviously Peter did comprehend that God was telling him that Gentiles were to receive the blessings of the gospel, for he opened his message in Cornelius's house by declaring he now understood that God does not show partiality in the dissemination of the gospel (10:34-35).

While no individual or church could touch every race in its witness or giving, this principle certainly forbids deliberately ignoring any group.

In the life of the church. Impartiality should also characterize certain basic aspects of church life and activity.

No one should be disqualified from being a leader in the church because of race. The church at Antioch exemplified racial impartiality since one of their leaders was Simeon whose nickname was Niger that means black. He was probably a Jew of African origin or possibly an African Gentile who was a proselyte to Judaism (Acts 13:1).

James sounded a warning as much needed today as in his time about showing partiality to those who are rich when they come into the assembly. Often they are offered a prominent place while a poor man, if he should come in, is asked to sit in an inconspicuous place. James says such partiality shows a false value system (James 2:3); it fails to honor the poor whom God honors (v. 5); it shows preference toward those who oppress (v. 6); and it is plainly sin (v. 9).

104

Professed interest in the poor of the world is clearly belied by courting the rich at home.

The questions of slavery. It is against this background of impartiality that the slavery question should be considered. Slavery was a part of the texture of first-century society, and it was of the most oppressive character.

> Kind and considerate masters were no doubt to be found; but the nature of the system permitted the grossest cruelties, and, as always in such cases, selfishness and brutality often took advantage of the permission. Slaves had practically no legal rights. . . . In persons thus situated who became Christians it was obviously natural in the highest degree that the assurance of their freedom in Christ would lead to such thoughts as these: "Can it possibly be that I, Christ's freedman, a citizen of the heavenly kingdom, a child of God, am to remain the bondman of this heathen, himself a slave of Satan?" Of course, supposing the master to be a Christian, the slave's thought would naturally be, "Since he and I are brethren, and therefore, even if he fail to see his duty in the matter, I have a right to assert my freedom and leave him, or should I remain in his house, claim in everything the equality of a brother." [Robert Johnstone, *The First Epistle of Peter (Edinburgh: T. & T. Clark, 1888), p. 166]*

Many try to make a case for the abolition of slavery from the direct teaching of the New Testament. However, a more accurate assessment of the matter is this: "Paul has no word of criticism for the institution as such. In this sense, he was unconcerned about 'social ethics'—the impact of the gospel on social structures" (George E. Ladd, *A Theology of the New Testament* [Grand Rapids:

105

Eerdmans, 1974], p. 529). However, Paul does say something about prejudice and impartiality that applies to the slavery question. Masters are warned against using their position to threaten their slaves on the basis that God is impartial (Ephesians 6:9), and when Paul sent the runaway slave Onesimus back to his master Philemon, he reminded Philemon to receive him as a brother, although he did not ask him to set Onesimus free (Philemon 16).

Why not?

If one single word from Christian teaching could have been quoted at Rome as tending to excite the slaves to revolt, it would have set the Roman Power in direct and active hostility to the new faith. Had St. Paul's teaching led (as it probably would, had he argued the cessation of servitude) to a rising of the slaves—that rising and the Christian Church, which would have been identified with it, would have been crushed together. Rome would not have tolerated a repetition of those servile wars which had, twice in the previous century, deluged Sicily with blood.

Nor would the danger of preaching the abolition of servitude have been confined to that arising from external violence on the part of the Roman Government; it would have been pregnant with danger to the purity of the Church itself. Many might have been led, from wrong motives, to join a communion which would have aided them in securing their social and political freedom.

In these considerations we may find, I think, ample reasons for the position of non-interference which the Apostle maintains in regard to slavery. If men then say that Christianity approved of slavery, we would point

106

them to the fact that it is Christianity that has abolished it. Under a particular and exceptional condition of circumstances, which cannot again rise, St. Paul, for wise reasons, did not interfere with it. To have done so would have been worse than useless. [T. Teignmouth Shore, "The First Epistle to the Corinthians," *A Bible Commentary for English Readers,* edited by C. J. Ellicott (London: Cassell, n.d.), 7: 310-11]

Thus, Paul's approach to this evil was to exhort believers, slave and free alike, to live like citizens of the new age within the structure of the soon-passing age.

Chapter Fourteen

An Agenda

An Agenda

Every person follows some agenda for his life. The goal of the believer ought to be to follow God's agenda as revealed in His Word.

The world also proposes an agenda for the Christian to follow. It eliminates redemption, or at least downgrades it. It focuses on society rather than the church. It finds success in statistics, not faithfulness. It glorifies man's abilities, not God's power.

The framework for the agenda. The biblical framework of history is a premillennial one, and any proper agenda must be constructed within that framework. This often provokes the charge that premillennialists are unconcerned about social problems since they believe the age will

111

climax with terrible apostasy. What's the use then of trying to better conditions in a doomed world? The Bible does teach that the church will become apostate, that world conditions will worsen, and that there will be no lasting peace until Christ returns to inaugurate His millennial kingdom. The Bible also commands doing good to all people and being salt and light. There is nothing inherent in premillennialism that causes insensitivity to the world around us. Some premillennialists may isolate themselves, but so do some with other or no eschatological views. Sound doctrine (which premillennialism is) is never the cause of wrong actions. People are.

In viewing the coming of Christ and the ultimate triumph of His rule, premillennialists are optimistic. But we are not so optimistic (or unbiblical) as to think that we can do now for the world what only Christ can do when He returns to establish righteousness. In viewing the present and future scene up to the time of His return, we are pessimistic. But we are not so pessimistic (or unbiblical) as to sit on our hands and do nothing to combat evil. In other words, we are both optimistic and pessimistic, which is biblical realism.

The expected end of life is death; but when I am sick I fight to prolong life, and when I am well I try to create conditions to keep well. The world is passing away (1 John 2:17), but I fight to bring the message of eternal life to that dying world and to create conditions in which the gospel may be better promoted.

The model for the agenda. One of the popular models for social action is the so-called incarnational model. In a word it is this: just as God performed His great work in the world through the incarnation of Christ, so now He continues that work through Christians in whom Christ is continually incarnated. Just as God was in Christ

112

coming to the rescue of the world, so now Christ is in us to rescue the world.

Although the idea is not entirely unscriptural, it is inept. The incarnation is the eternal Word become flesh. Christ's indwelling of believers is in no sense His becoming flesh again. The means of the incarnation was the virgin birth; after the resurrection, the humanity of Christ was a risen and glorified humanity. The incarnational model seems to imply that the present form of the humanity of Christ is our bodies which He indwells. But that is not so. His present form is described in Revelation 1 and 5, His body being wounded and risen. That Christ lives in and works through believers is indisputable, but not because of any incarnation in believers.

A much more accurate model is the servant model. The incarnation resulted in Christ's taking the form of a servant, and that example is held up to believers to follow (Philippians 2; 1 Peter 2:21; 1 John 2:6). But to clarify the concept two questions need to be considered: (1) Why did Christ become a servant? and (2) To whom did He become a servant?

1. Christ became a servant in order to die. That self-sacrificing love is the example believers are to follow (John 13:1-17; 1 Peter 2:21; 1 John 2:6). That does not mean that if we cannot give our lives for someone else then we are relieved of obligation. John makes it clear that few will be called on to do that, but all can show self-sacrificing love by giving to other Christians (1 John 3:15-16).

Peter relates the servant concept to the obedience of slaves to their masters, whether unsaved or saved (1 Peter 2:18-21). In Philippians 2 Paul likens the work that he, Timothy, and Epaphroditus had done to the self-sacrificing service of the Lord.

113

Concretely, service means (a) giving to other believers, (b) doing your job well as a testimony, and (c) sacrificial service for the Lord's work.

2. Whom do we serve? The answer of the New Testament is loud and clear: you serve the Lord Christ (Colossians 3:24). But what has happened in the thinking of some is a kind of mutation whereby the servant of the Lord becomes the servant of the world. "The practical conclusion to which this leads, in practice if not in theory, is that the church now takes its cues from the world. Casting herself in the role of servant, the church, perhaps unthinkingly, has cast the world in the role of master" (Larry Christenson, *A Charismatic Approach to Social Action* [Minneapolis: Bethany, 1974], p. 102).

Scripture is crystal clear: Christ is our master, not the world, and we take our orders and agenda from Him. Imitating Christ means doing those things that please the Father (John 8:29). Christenson continues: "The church *is* sent into the world to serve—sent by the Lord. But that is quite another thing from being called *by the world.* The list of needs which the world sets for itself may be quite different than the priorities which God sets for it. The church serves the world only at those places and in those ways and toward those ends which God may determine" (ibid., p. 103).

I have tried to describe those ways along with their respective priorities in the preceding chapters.

Items for the agenda.

1. At the top of the list I would put the cultivation of personal holiness. It is more important to be than to do, for if I am what God wants me to be, then I will do what He wants me to do. If I try to promote a program, however well-meaning, without personal holiness, it will be tainted by the

defects of my life. It may lack the direction of full knowledge of the Word, or the discernment of maturity, or the direction that comes through unclouded fellowship with the Lord. Primarily we do not need to develop programs, but people.

If that sounds too individualistic, pietistic, or isolationist, remember that this is the biblical emphasis. God's purpose is to perfect a people "having no spot or wrinkle or any such thing," but "holy and blameless" (Ephesians 5:27). The changing of individuals, not institutions, is primary.

> If we are horrified by the fact that we do not place the changing of institutions (property, distribution, administration, etc.) at the centre, it can only mean two things: either we are conscious Marxists, and do not believe in the existence of human *nature,* but only in the existence of a human *condition,* which can be wholly and radically modified by changing institutions . . . or, on the other hand, we are hypocrites, and we are refusing . . . to look at the heart of man, and are simply considering his environment. [Jacques Ellul, *The Presence of the Kingdom* (Philadelphia: Westminster, 1951), p. 84]

2. Be vitally concerned and involved in spreading the gospel. This is our biblical mandate. This was the example of the early church whose primary concern was to spread the good news. It recognizes man's most basic and serious need, and it offers the only solution to his eternal welfare. It simply is not true that you cannot preach the gospel to a hungry person. Indeed, you had better preach it to him, for he might die of starvation before you or anyone could save his life. And then where would he be?

Our evangelical congresses and conventions

often include some breast-beating and confession for not having met the material needs of our fellow man. If that be in order, how much more would be in order heartbreaking confession for not having met the spiritual needs of the world? Planning, strategy, and corporate effort have their place in reaching the world with the gospel, but our needs are usually not in those areas. Individual believers simply need to pray for unsaved friends, need to be sensitive to opportunities, and need to give more generously. We do not need more conventions, but more commitment; not more congresses, but more concern; not more methods, but more motivation; not more programs, but more prayer.

3. Be involved in building Christ's church. To do this is to add new converts to His body. To do this is to mature believers. To do this is to erect a model of love and concern that will attract unbelievers to the truth (John 13:34). To do this is to be involved in all kinds of supportive activities with other believers (Hebrews 10:24; James 5:16; 1 John 3:17). And to do all these things will necessitate dependence on and the demonstration of the power of the Holy Spirit.

4. Strive for a generous life-style. Much is written concerning simplified life-styles for Christians and some of the exhortations are very much in order. It is really not possible to list universal standards for all believers, for what might be a proper simplified life for one could be an improper extravagant life for another. Yet there are restraints that could likely be employed by most: living within a balanced budget, credit cards for thirty-day convenience only, ignoring faddish trends, driving a car less and longer, making do instead of buying new, and so on.

However, we may have been looking at the wrong side of the problem when we concentrate on what we can eliminate from our life-styles. We should be looking at the other side, seeking ways we can be increasingly generous. In other words, if one deliberately seeks ways to increase his giving he will also find ways to cut expenses so that he will have more to give. I am not speaking of increasing income in order to be able to give more, but increasing the percentage available for giving from whatever income one has.

A generous life of giving will also redirect the use of time, redeeming it for service of others rather than self. That, in turn, may simplify one's life-style and even release some additional money for others.

These suggestions about life-style can apply to believers in all economic brackets. And the Lord does place His children in different economic situations in His will.

Perspectives on the agenda. Whatever items you place on your agenda, may I remind you of two important considerations about them.

1. Responsibility is individual even if it relates to a cooperative or group activity. Concerted activity is biblical, but it is only as good as the effort each one puts into it. Ultimately it is the individual's responsible actions that produce results, whether they are done person-to-person or through the church, parachurch organizations, or other entities.

2. Biblical priorities must never be adjusted or abandoned. As believers we do have clear priorities with respect to godliness, evangelism, church and social responsibilities. It is my hope that this study has helped put them in a clearer light.